Brachiosaurus

by Daniel Cohen

Consultant:
Brent Breithaupt
Director
Geological Museum
University of Wyoming

Bridgestone Books
an imprint of Capstone Press
Mankato, Minnesota

Bridgestone Books are published by Capstone Press
151 Good Counsel Drive, P.O. Box 669, Mankato, Minnesota 56002
http://www.capstone-press.com

Library of Congress Cataloging-in-Publication Data
Cohen, Daniel, 1936–
    Brachiosaurus / by Daniel Cohen.
    p. cm.—(Discovering dinosaurs)
    Summary: Describes what is known about the physical characteristics, behavior, and habitat of this very large dinosaur.
    Includes bibliographical references and index.
    ISBN 0-7368-1620-8 (hardcover)
    1. Brachiosaurus—Juvenile literature. [1. Brachiosaurus. 2. Dinosaurs.] I. Title.
QE862.S3 C5614 2003
567.913—dc21   2002010558

Editorial Credits
Erika Shores, editor; Karen Risch, product planning editor; Linda Clavel, series designer;
    Patrick D. Dentinger, cover production designer; Angi Gahler, production artist;
    Alta Schaffer, photo researcher

Photo Credits
Corbis, cover, 1; Bob Krist, 8
Index Stock Imagery/RO-MA Stock, 6
James P. Rowan, 16
Steven Brusatte/Dino Land Paleontology, 10
The Natural History Museum, 14; Orbis, 4, 12, 20

1 2 3 4 5 6 08 07 06 05 04 03

Table of Contents

Brachiosaurus compared to a
5-foot-tall (1.5-meter-tall) human

Brachiosaurus

Brachiosaurus (BRAK-ee-oh-SORE-us) belonged to a group of dinosaurs called sauropods (SORE-oh-pods). Sauropods were the largest dinosaurs ever to live. Brachiosaurus stood 39 to 50 feet (12 to 15 meters) tall. It weighed 33 to 88 tons (30 to 80 metric tons).

The World of Brachiosaurus

Brachiosaurus lived about 150 million years ago. Earth looked different during this time. Earth's landmasses were closer together. The climate was warm and wet. Many plants such as ferns and gingkos covered the land.

gingko
a tree with green, fan-shaped leaves

Barosaurus was a relative of Brachiosaurus. Both Brachiosaurus and Barosaurus were sauropods.

Relatives of Brachiosaurus

Many kinds of sauropods lived at the
time of Brachiosaurus. Apatosaurus
(ah-PAT-oh-SORE-us) and Barosaurus
(BAR-oh-SORE-us) were two large
sauropods.

nostril

tail

Parts of Brachiosaurus

Brachiosaurus means "arm lizard." Its front arms were longer than its back legs. Brachiosaurus had a long neck, thick body, and long tail. Brachiosaurus could breathe through nostrils on the top of its head.

What Brachiosaurus Ate

Brachiosaurus was a herbivore. It only ate plants. Brachiosaurus could eat the leaves off the tops of trees. Brachiosaurus had a small mouth. Scientists think Brachiosaurus ate all of the time in order to stay alive.

Predators

Many meat-eating dinosaurs lived during the time of Brachiosaurus. Allosaurus (AL-oh-SORE-rus) was one of these dinosaurs. But Allosaurus was too small to attack an adult Brachiosaurus. Allosaurus sometimes attacked a young or sick Brachiosaurus.

End of Brachiosaurus

Brachiosaurus and some other sauropods became extinct 125 million years ago. Dinosaurs continued to live on Earth for another 60 million years. None of the other dinosaurs were as big as the sauropods.

extinct
no longer living anywhere in the world

Wyoming

Utah Colorado

UNITED STATES

TANZANI

☐ Areas where Brachiosaurus
fossils have been found

Discovering Brachiosaurus

The first Brachiosaurus fossil was found
in Colorado in 1900. Brachiosaurus
fossils also have been found in Wyoming
and Utah. German scientists found
Brachiosaurus fossils in east Africa. The
most complete Brachiosaurus skeleton
is on display in Berlin, Germany.

Studying Brachiosaurus Today

Paleontologists once thought Brachiosaurus was too big to walk on land. They thought Brachiosaurus spent most of its time in the water. They now think Brachiosaurus and other large sauropods did live on land. They may have traveled together in large herds.

herd
a group of animals; sauropods may have traveled in herds.

Hands On: How Tall Was Brachiosaurus?

Brachiosaurus' head reached 39 feet (12 meters) off the ground. If the dinosaur lived today it could look over the top of a four-story building. This activity will show you the height of Brachiosaurus.

What You Need

A large, open area
Masking tape
Tape measure
A friend

What You Do

1. Mark a spot on the floor with a piece of masking tape.
2. Measure 39 feet (12 meters) on the floor. Mark the spot with another piece of tape.
3. Start at one end. Placing one foot in front of the other, count how many steps it takes you to get to the other end.
4. Now, have your friend lie on the ground. Place a piece of tape on the ground to mark where his or her head and feet are.
5. Have your friend stand up. Count the steps as you walk from the tape marking your friend's head to the tape marking your friend's feet. How many more steps did you take in Step 3?

Words to Know

climate (KLYE-mit)—the usual weather in a place

dinosaur (DYE-na-sore)—an extinct land reptile; dinosaurs lived on Earth for more than 150 million years.

fossil (FOSS-uhl)—the remains or traces of something that once lived; bones and footprints can be fossils.

gingko (GING-koh)—a tree with green, fan-shaped leaves

herbivore (HUR-buh-vor)—an animal that eats only plants

paleontologist (PAY-lee-on-TOL-ah-jist)— a scientist who finds and studies fossils

predator (PRED-a-tur)—an animal that hunts other animals for food

scientist (SYE-uhn-tist)—a person who studies the world around us

Read More

Benton, Michael. *Giant Plant Eaters.* Awesome Dinosaurs. Brookfield, Conn.: Copper Beech Books, 2001.

Goecke, Michael P. *Brachiosaurus.* A Buddy Book. Edina, Minn.: Abdo, 2002.

Oliver, Rupert. *Brachiosaurus.* Dinosaur Library. Vero Beach, Fla.: Rourke, 2001.

Internet Sites

Track down many sites about Brachiosaurus.
Visit the FACT HOUND at *http://www.facthound.com*

IT IS EASY! IT IS FUN!

1) Go to *http://www.facthound.com*
2) Type in: 0736816208
3) Click on "FETCH IT" and FACT HOUND will find several links hand-picked by our editors.

Relax and let our pal FACT HOUND do the research for you!

Index